Sports

I Can Go Hiking

By Edana Eckart

Children's Press®
A Division of Scholastic Inc.
New York / Toronto / London / Auckland / Sydney
Mexico City / New Delhi / Hong Kong
Danbury, Connecticut

Photo Credits: Cover and all photos by Maura B. McConnell
Contributing Editor: Jennifer Silate
Book Design: Mindy Liu

Library of Congress Cataloging-in-Publication Data

Eckart, Edana.
  I can go hiking / by Edana Eckart.
  p. cm. — (Sports)
  Includes index.
  Summary: When a father and son go hiking, the young boy shows the reader
  how to have fun exploring nature properly and safely.
  ISBN 0-516-24276-8 (lib. bdg.) — ISBN 0-516-24368-3 (pbk.)
  1. Hiking—Juvenile literature. [1. Hiking.] I. Title.

  GV199.52 .E35 2003
  796.51—dc21

                                                    2002007939

Contents

My name is Sam.

Today, my dad and I are going **hiking** in the **park**.

I wear **boots** and long pants to go hiking.

I also wear a hat.

7

Dad will carry a **backpack** on our hike.

He puts water and food in his backpack.

We are ready to go hiking.

Dad will drive us to
the park.

We are at the park.

We will hike on a **trail**.

13

There are blue **signs** on these trees.

The blue signs tell us that we are on the trail.

We see many plants on our hike.

There is a flower.

It is a **dandelion**.

We see many plants
on our hike.

There is a flower.

It is a **dandelion**.

It is time to rest.

I drink some of the water we brought.

We are at the end
of the trail.

Hiking is fun!

21

New Words

backpack (**bak**-pak) a cloth bag worn on the back, used to carry things you want to take with you

boots (**boots**) heavy shoes that cover your ankles and sometimes part of your legs

dandelion (**dan**-duh-lie-uhn) a small plant with a yellow flower and green leaves

hiking (**hike**-ing) going on a long walk

park (**park**) an area of land with trees, benches, and sometimes playgrounds, used by the public for recreation

signs (**sinez**) symbols that stand for something

trail (**trayl**) a track or path for people to follow, especially in the woods

To Find Out More

Books
Exploring Parks with Ranger Dockett
by Alice K. Flanagan
Children's Press

Trekking on a Trail: Hiking Adventures for Kids
by Linda White
Gibbs Smith Publisher

Web Site
Kids' Domain: Ecosports
http://www.kidsdomain.com/sports/camp/
Learn about first aid, read hiking stories, and find out about other outdoor sports on this Web site.

Index

backpack, 8

boots, 6

dandelion, 16

hat, 6

hiking, 4, 6, 10

park, 4, 10, 12

signs, 14

trail, 12, 14, 20

water, 8, 18

About the Author

Edana Eckart has written several children's books. She enjoys bike riding with her family.

Reading Consultants

Kris Flynn, Coordinator, Small School District Literacy, The San Diego County Office of Education

Shelly Forys, Certified Reading Recovery Specialist, W.J. Zahnow Elementary School, Waterloo, IL

Sue McAdams, Former President of the North Texas Reading Council of the IRA, and Early Literacy Consultant, Dallas, TX